# POEMS
*without*
# IRONY

—

*Alex* WONG

CARCANET

First published in Great Britain in 2016 by
CARCANET PRESS LTD
Alliance House, 30 Cross Street
Manchester M2 7AQ
www.carcanet.co.uk

A CIP catalogue record for this book is available
from the British Library: ISBN 9781784103040

Designed by Luke Allan.
Printed and bound in England by SRP Ltd.

The publisher acknowledges financial assistance
from Arts Council England.

# CONTENTS

Nooks are also by the tideless sea where a rock bars the way, and nooks in the bays where only a boat can enter. But wherever they are, and under whatever sky, they are the figures of certain regions of human thought through which there is no passage. An enclosure not of imprisonment, a finality not of despair are at the end of such thoughts; there is no way beyond, there is no knowledge to reach, there is no explanation, and if a question leads thither there is no solution . . .

ALICE MEYNELL

'I'd give almost anything to be blasé.'

RONALD FIRBANK

These
poems are
designed to be
read using the mouth

POEMS WITHOUT IRONY

# SIX CONSOLATIONS

## *Consolation № 1*

Supposing Hell a thick facsimile;——
    At least a long tomorrow, dropping
Footnotes to this evening.

Then, what to hope?
    the choice?
        or a final sleep—

A second death: between today undying,
And some impeccable substance not disturbed
By argument or love?

I wait. And I'll get sick, and you be pretty.
        I think I am damned already:
As your approval came with harrowing light.

If only balance seemed to be enough.

                *

Now everything is startlingly dear.
I need that sense of pressure, need
Unnecessary dressing of new friendship,—

        Making novel notes, giving
                Version, variation;
        Humane philologies
        Of harsh mechanical day;—
                Scribbled evening, too,
        and naked morning;—

Your most unlikely wonderful resource.

But I'm most cute as a rather chaotic being,—
Taken, attached; whose only will strikes out
      For you,    to you,    leaping.

Euphoric disorder opening for a day?
      Best offer,    and I'm ready;

But then, high massive walls, made out of you,
      Let me,    check me.

*

Still preparing the same old kind of lie?
Greek obsession lying by,
About——to spring out——on schedule?

But then, this evening, would you include me? I'm
Late, deservedly.    But you
Are marked this time.——

*

Oh, Feeling cakes against my *thinking things*.
But just what no
Broodings    are found able to explain,

Tomorrow might assuage;
When, ends being given over,
Cut letters, though they do not quite

Control the finer needs—the delight
Never had; the thing never done; the result
Today never sent,—

Could get together and make,
From between you     and my unstable living,
Some calm, in correlations.

Yet, the first little minute filling up
Evening with white thanks,

I see you're back with struggle in my mind;
Far from my reasons in the knowing day.

*

And I'll be trying, in any case;
    In any degree, *trying*—
    And likely boring;—
Because these pictures will not double for you.

My prurience
    flowers
        in academic editions,

Brought to bed
    excerpted;
        they won't state

My thought but by suggestion.
                            Good enough?

*

Let me send you some small, sleepy gift.
        Here is that 'human love'—
Heard better now, because the howling distance:
It must get real, get realising, be
Reconstituted. Must be *obvious*.

. . . To pound the cliffs
Like a sea? The chronic repeats,
Feeding rubble of chalk into the salt,
Might only make tomorrow turn inland—

Away from dealing with
            the sense I want to make,

And all delighted dealing of my sense.


*


I have much need of cool declension,
Generation of things in regular form.
Give me a word to meet my little speech—?

The sound swims back unbroken:
                              back from you,
To meet me, marking time
            with nails on level tables.

She dropped a subtle plummet.
     In the lines
Of a mask
     as in the patterns of a rug
She lost it;     in the contours
     of a shrug, a tilt.    And still

Continued to be given love;

         but felt
A Psyche, errant
     in the street outside—
Or inside, though blindfolded
        with a cloth
Tied up    as firm as
     death by suicide;

While a thin laugh went rummaging in the blank
     Between their limits:
Among the pulls, the ambitions—
Through all the formal torpor of an old

And only metaphysical Versailles;
       She comes against the bête,
The inert;    the desperate art, the sliding wit.

It is not turbulent;    it is not stark.

He bounded through his times in retrospect
And came away uncomprehending,
    cold.
Still we continue to be given love.——

Should waters without shape,
      with crooked thoughts, encroach,
Come beyond that strong
      new railing; pass across
Proud inches of the lip;
      under the painted door;
And play about my bed—
            (then comes the mould. . .)

I have no screen against     these wavering forces.
No lock sustained inviolate!
      neither inglorious decoy.
The waters approach,     there is no mending.

           *

And I do not expect     difficult grace.
But should a blessing prove upon me, carry
Whispers of intimate ease,
      our own familiar things,

   I'll be
   No scrambling Daphne.

   _____

   No kiss
   Will chase back morning,

Knock current air again into the night,—
The nauseous province that the squeezing mind
Passes in a secrecy of love.

I banish things I miss;
      let us be strange again.

*

Or will you bear
To bring your gentle bid
     up to the verge,

To that Good other creature? Can you dare
Suppose the one end,
     the one sworn want
         that love seems not to have met,

Was hardly everything? Allow it now.

And those remembered interrogatories,
    Contrived to the moment's fashion,
    Enlarged under the humour
Of solitude and these pedantic hours,

Won't diminish all
     our common dominion
(This contented court
    as it was before);

Shall not exceed
     shut doors of a home *agreed*,—
Absent from,    or could we say it, freed
     from tedious atlases . . .

So let the curious look for us,
Missing together,    lacing together.
                Only,
I am not well assured.
         Stay, pretty foot;——

*

I pick at bones
Till trifles signify
Impossible hope:

Bounty with artifice bred
Of cant—let out in all
We said—and gall unshed.

*

Speak me a house; propose the time, the measure.
Think yourself *out*——advanced,
        into a simple morning:
Somewhere for another liberty,——
Foreign to this spectrum I denounce
As slumbers are which don't dwindle at day.

Never the question admitted
        of the degrees discarded.

Dwell for a little period;
        some month: let it be May.
And stop all feedback from the native scene;
Prohibit all referral to the commerce
Of reasonable tomorrows.
                    But you wait,

I feel you waiting at the abbey grate:
Friend—of the many baskets;—
        chariot always oiled,
Ready for the faithful long pursuit—?

And do I run away till I submit?

I went after something,
    Eager to seem busy;
Not talking but just going.

I turn uphill,
      write this;

The phone-line is frayed.

          \*

The ghosts are in the garden,
          our old garden;

Where happened, and which itself was
         all the matter

Of myths we must and cannot correlate
With the new bodies touching our new bodies—

Whose gardens
     were somewhere else.
  Descriptions
     dull in the ear.

          \*

I find you in the maidenhair,
The hip-bone lines along the leaf,
And the trees' pert poses,
         even on days without wind;
And, most, in the desire
     to make an observation;—

I turn downhill,
    write this—

To the old address.

      *

We do not make
The smell of morning,

Which does
More than you know

To paint out
The disingenuousness

Of evening.

      *

Is this
    a trickling well,
Under
    the wooden frame

You and I
    make together,
Propped
    on the level time?

The planning;—just two wardrobes, and the bed;
You preface everything
      with a sense of need.

Yes, I'd have room,
      and time—the dark time surely—
For any possibilities of touch;
For more than christening nerves in both of us.

\*

I'm going at your thing—your own;
    Immeasurably you;
Huge pack of hope—with hope, till all
    Your places I couldn't already

Think, have seen I'm here,—
      and come for the best, I hope.

\*

The only sphere,
    This calm between itself,
Passes to murmur
    And lonely sleep.

Landing, with new means,
    This time I will enquire
Even more difficult things;

Stride the rustling night,
    Rolling warm little downs—
On my deep night visit.

*

But then, the departure—do I miss some love?
    And when I have to be going,
Saving up the fantasies downstairs,
    And day shall course right on,—

    You're quickly put just there;
And my stuff person petrified apart.

*

And so I tend the night mess;
    Though to no sure effect.

There is a good even there;
    It feels like moving.

Before the sympathy given,—
Find out this other One,
          which also is much;

More than oneself     it may be;
      more than one:—

Who has been—for sure—concerned
In passionate relations,
          perhaps not wholly over;

Unknown corresponding friend,
      Frankly at my side,
Making the moorhen on the bank

A more mysterious agent     in my world.

                    *

The least of what can be discovered
Tacitly suggesting you;
Any old making into self
          —barely then regarded—

This lonely comb
          which was exactly *there*
And now is here, more heavily it seems,

In quiet associative vitality
Declaring
          something
                    had.

(That small thing happened once,
      And through, and through . . .)

But meeting
     everything
         that came for us,
Have we
     dominated
         the event?


\*


Like space around the waking of the mind,
     Flash out around me now,
         Be door, be wardrobe,—

Glow around the window;
Glasses, glass of water,
         switch for light.

Surround me,
     like the sudden rain outside

When, in the dark,
         retracted to the head,
Elsewhere, or nowhere, I've known—

Until that soft expansion of the ken
Includes the street,
         the garden,
     and the water—
Only as further bounding, and as blurred,
As numb,
     as that near bounding of the skull.

*

For the sense more solid of a subject not
Subject to me,
        Nor for its life pertaining,

First there needs
        Decision, the cut
Of an object——apart from the meaning
                Habit
                Throws about——?

Sense of the object:    not mine, never me;
From which the autonomous agency
Like a miracle rises
                in my way.

# IDYLL

Brushing your hair on the landing, out of sight,
     While the late dream state
Steams off me like water
From the shell an egg just boiled;—

You remind me of what perhaps
     I was half in mind of,
The other day, when that
Well-favoured cow,

Declining its fleecy
Jowls, so gently
Ripped up the delicate tufts.    Oh, Shepherdess——
     *Brunch*—?—?

# CLUNK

By the side of the road there came a flattish sense
Of something too familiar—with a clunk,
Like heavy doors on classic Cadillacs.
Was there charlatanry in my confession?

The highland cow, sitting beside the fence,
A silent but a sedulous quidnunc,
Encumbered in her melancholy locks,
Was shaggy and sad as Alfred Tennyson.

Like a fanfare of silver harpsichords
The moon was in full cry on the black woods
And rang metallic round our haloed pates.

Confected moments in heraldic state
Stood, romantic and rigid, like tapestry birds,
Among the wet lamps—and fly away, now, backwards.

A pheasant wriggles into the air / the car
Passes under its steep diagonal.
With the wet grass,
              in a ridge down to the tail,
Ripple the dry parts of a badger's fur;—

Dark, spiny mouth agape—malevolent,
Taut ellipse... The pigeon starts again,
One long, one short:
              a slow, two-tone refrain;
*Fouettés*, though turned in some denser element.

The pheasant is steady; the long plumes trail and quiver
Behind;—tail-lights, and the sun along the chrome,
Flash on the rise
              and dip out; the bees' hum
Misgiven, as two round blue-tits jounce and dither.

As if you were gliding overhead,
    Deep in the woods my cargo cult
    Still imprecates the thunder bolt
To bring you down upon the bed.

But faith in fortune has been tricked
    Too often. Now you're overpaved
    And cold—like all I thought I'd saved—
And hope lies under interdict.

And my suspicious scholiast
    Is busy asking what it meant.
    His commentaries thereanent
Strain to will down the fugitive past.

# LINES WRITTEN UPON HEARING THAT 'DIPPY' THE DINOSAUR WOULD BE REPLACED BY AN AUTHENTIC WHALE

*'only a plaster cast'*

I did not know the enormous dinosaur
Standing entire inside the entrance hall
Of the NATURAL HISTORY MUSEUM in London

Was known affectionately as 'Dippy'
    (i.e. from *diplodocus*);
But these lines

Were written on hearing of plans to take it away.
Like everyone else, I was much aggrieved,
        and I wrote these lines.

The flinches I remember:
       Straining away    from a man's conducive hand
That led toward the unpredictable lizard.
Original terror made
For a care that only now resuscitates.

It was a person    a very big one
It was not like me
We did not correlate.

We came to terms, though agency remained
    Undisclosed.
Visits repeated: there was so much relation;
Only one other I mind of,——and that was the panda.
      (The hand I put out of mind, I am making
      Contrast, not equation.)

Now I discover you do correlate. I have
   Found something for you;—
Because you were a great Object, and always I gave you credit
   For a secret Being
In excess of what might have seemed available.

If I am the nice new Lady of the land
And smuggle pretty loaves down to the village,
I am also the jealous husband by the way.

I smuggle the bread from our table. And I
    Resent it;
    Or find it——unbefitting;
    Or fear,
At any rate, what the kith and kin may say.

From chilly clasping arms
    Hang down, beneath the pelt,
Snug lumps—a gravid burden, warm—
    Bellying out the pleats.

But, roses?    Now?    At *this* time of the year?
Already I have more than half confessed
When the scent flicks out, on the sting of frosty air . . .

Am I the deity? If a third person passed,
What would the hard light show on the printed track,
    Spilled
                From the skirts let fall?    Flowers only, there?

———

Rambler, direct your care
    To this magnificent gift.
Dare, rambler, to make durable those views.


——More trust, believe, more debit.——


Lest the day come to see all trust is up,
Learn to speak newly over nature; build
Fresh castles for your chances to enjoy.
    Make chiffchaffs pay to find a way
Within, from a world not edified since Eden.


Hear in the song not only expressive bird,
But a history in your tongue, to beat the bounds.
As a child skims the ways of ideal gardens,
    So can you then,    so have you those
Adventures to go on with, grounds
Possible to their keepers;—outworks, follies.

Had faults and fears been *entre nous*,
It would all be different now. Slowly emerges
Some new glamour, trained on you—
And I, though frighted by the mounting burgess,
Hid my distemper
That flat November . . .
Green shoots, and I grope at you for purchase.

What, *really*? For your paragon,
That imbecilic bullshit mountebank?
I, where the faerie people wonne,
Retire to exile—one more comedy crank
Crossing the border;
The old order
Haunting the marches, till the nail and plank.

The best of you and the worst of you
He will not see distinct. It will all be the same
To him—first new, and then not new—
A shame to both of you. But more my shame.
Come to the test
What was best
I can now, but I could not number or name.

I know it now! And how could *he* know,
Full of his grisly swagger—this bright gaud?
So I, the hapless Pedrolino,
Feigning amazement you could be so awed
By the pied prick,
Flee the stick
To nurse, alone, the blows—and my slender hoard.

# PROTECTION

Relieved myself with a handful
    Of tractable situations;—
Dressing the room in vanity
      To mask a reluctant pleasure.—
        Unreassuring night-lights,
        Your far eyes tell on me,
And spoil my poor, but various, new endeavours.

This and that mask: one moulded
    Over the awkward child;—
And that more fearsome one
      Is a local nameless spirit . . .
        I use—I need protection;
        But if you would submit me
To a more aggressive scrutiny, I could bear it.

Then came you, being in love with
        gloom, profound recess,
To the emulation of the grand sublime,
            Saying:

You shall understand that greatly
I have esteemed
Vermillion little lips bordering
        China hard,
                Against china soft;

But now pacific stone marks out my store
In spaces which are answerable to mine.

Of which the top part came down,
Twice even.
(And then once more.)

There remains the porcelain and the whole classical thing.
The Bellini with buttons like sea-snails,—
                    The nautilus shells,
The Raphael, the clarid line.

Further reflective years succeeded;
Brought you,
        after many impeding thunders,
'As though by an unseen agency',
To the deep retirement,
                stilling of that level;

The sheets and pillars of granite (I
  Remembered it black, but it was pink);
The glossy, continent tomb

Deflecting every angle,
With a moat dug in the grass.

Even the full soil, this firm ground
Groans to an arch beneath our shoes
Like the face of a pie rising—

With all those bodies bundled
(How many *per* square metre).
Lungs breathing down in the compact earth
That weighs like water round the floating dead.

                              *

What things can punctuate a soul, or sting
        The nervous pore, like spirits, more
Than a dimple, uneven moving of the mouth,
        The heavy pinkness around your eyes;

        The grieving saints
        Are not so moving
As these, their drapery never so involving
        As that heavy pinkness,
        That falling and folding.

                              *

Will a face float up before me when I am drowning
(If, in the end, it happens) and the lungs
Fill up with your secular, mortal breath;—
Lifting limbs from the mirror, the surface, outward;—
Falling back to your more responsive waters;—
Drowning shyly, deliberately, being
*Drowned* at last . . .
                        Like a kitten in the sink;

But one whose lives are really nine
And stronger with every expiation. I am
No quietist, want to enjoy,
To see from every angle, taste
The salt, to show each snare
The hardness of irony,
The softness of compliance —
But no precautious piety, no waste.

*

I am still afraid
For in that faceless golden head
I see no eyes.

Her blond hair, her back to me,
The face I cannot see, pressed
Hard against another breast.

The blackness she sees
Is not the blankness I see
In that faceless golden head.

*

What if the ground simmers up around our legs —
Will it take us in, the dead slide round about us
Again? The ones with bullets in their backs;
The ones who wandered down there by mistake,
            Making a cup of tea;
Or those who had to use the forbidden key?

And will they be just like their photographs?
Their faces will be closed against the waters.

And even supposing the water should come to be
Fresh and cool and clear, seem sweet to savour,
Still as I bend to drink, I shall only see better
The crayfish scuttling in the rocks, and lobsters
Trailing strands of your hair in their grey hands,
Their colder-blooded, colder-blooded claws.

With sudden decision,
As when the head
   Of an owl
Mechanically swivels,

Water spouts
From the verdigris
   Of the sky's
Repoussé metal plate.

Inches from my face, the elbow
Of a corpulent lady relaxed to a wrinkle
Under the hem of a short grey sleeve. But I thought

Of those big, pale, pinguid Amalfi lemons!
The points peeping from the folds—
Soft peaks, solid in sun and rain.

Continental comparisons!
England smells so different in the sunshine;
O, there's enough to keep me
From lascivious agitations—
Till the afternoon, at any rate.

Sometimes, for a moment, I think——
——————————wouldn't it be nice . . .
Though, on the other hand, gratitude.

The sun shines, or it rains
(An even better smell);    casting around
For someone to thank,
I find only myself—
(Or you, Papagena!);

Query, is this why God made us
In his own image?

Between my face and the window,
The motes are passing in calm traffic
Like futuristic vehicles in Fritz Lang's *Metropolis*.

Very subtle seem the Spring's
      Achievements to the eye; and not
           Distent, as later, when the fruit
Is spent;—but to the brain, this crescent life
Weighs quite a lot, with all these little things.

It is like this: something sings——
      The measure I don't follow; so many
           Nouns; what else? I cannot parse
The period: sticky leaf, and tiny coot,
And milky blossoms of the open-arse.

Lozenges against the grass,
      Where the banks slope to the waters:
           Bright quenelles of raw meringue,
Stowing their heads, each one, beneath a wing.
So neat;—but all those furry sons and daughters!

In my little *hortus*
      *Conclusus*, the soil produces
           Broods of pointed little red
Tulips, gaping—chick-like—to be fed.
They gape still, when a bee comes for the juices.

Another one chooses
      To rifle the public daffodils. Humming fills
           The horn: the voice is found
For its empty shouting. To its empty shouting
Only the pollinating bee gives sound.

On the public ground
      Are many daisies. I understand

                    Better the meaning of
Their night-time looks, when candour scrunches close;—
Close, like fingers of a sprinkling hand.

About to land,
              The mallard now returning to the park
                    Curls-in his body, like a prawn.
The wide horse-chestnut sweeps the lawn
Like a girl's fringe. It is getting dark.

              Yes——to the torture-mark
Patterning of the path;—the cracks of the bark;
And the cracquelure of the dirt at the edge of the field,
              Ill annealed.

And so the Roman arriving army, six
After the battle years,
        of three divisions

Bones—
        no one knowing
        if strangers' relics
Or of their own, he covered in earth;
                                    yet all

As though those
        of their close    comrades;—
                as though

Those of their blood—
        swollen toward the opponent
Bitterness;
        sad at once,     and incensed,

——interred.

On a hot particular day
When the loose, broad spread of an iris,
   Blue, faint as a vein,

Like a long-time missed initial   in fancy majuscule,—
   Seemed, in generous lapse
      of limb, poised slack and easy,
Equal expression for all things of that day,—

This deeper blue,—reflex,
       faced fair in the shallow pool,—
Still wet, when we pass,
In the road, where the wagtail

    Bent,
    sharp,
    at the border
    to drink,—

Was asking to be furled in my rocaille;—
   Though I am on better terms with the frilled iris:
It is erotic; I know what to do with it.

Now he's deploying I do not so much
Covet the idiosyncrasies of touch.

In a dull light recur to me
The promptings of expectancy;

From which the fragments I retain
Could be Hallstatt or La Tène.

My reconstructed images of us
Are curious because so dubious;—

Call them Beaker people. We
Are about to engage in archaeology.

Something strange is lurching over,
Stiff as a hanged man, juddering closer . . .

We did all we could to inaugurate
This coalition—puppet state;—

And now my tired, reluctant antipope
Throws a cool eye on the auspices of hope.

# INTRICACY

## Hendecasyllabics

### I.

Veins and arteries make a tense commotion;
New half-seconds are thrown among the moments—
Cries arriving around again, and clutching
Hands;
   one serpentine figure, two intentions.

Half a minute of stupor without contact
Scores an orchestra silence cannot still, that
Scowls, continues.
     And in his lifted alcove,
Pointing down to the squirmers, bright Apollo
Says:
  You wanted a good time;
        *have a bad time.*

### II.

Calmly written, another abject letter:
Slow-paced, celibate, stately (just like his, but
Better).

   This is what all the sickness comes to.
Four sheets. Burn before reading. Blow the relics
Lightly over your palm.
     In that sufflation
Make me wither by sympathetic magic.

No trace more of the old, love-talking cross-eye,
Limping, dragging his head,
      two steps behind you.

# THE DISAPPOINTMENT

## Asclepiadics

Crates, prised open and left, empty and splintery,
Lie slant over the curb, lit by a conical
Reach of yellow the rain's steady obliquity
Catches,    glinting its grain,    tilting.

                                    The sediment
Failure throws in the night's pitiful homecoming—
That dark silt, with its glint—sticks in the gullet and
Clogs. Night dredges the pool. Morning is rancorous.

Smell of fish by the drains;    yesterday, market day,
Fresh clear ice, and the sole, turbot and halibut;
Lobsters, prawns; and the bright    herring, recumbent and
Slick.

        The butcher was here, poured in the gutter his
Pails of water, made red; tainted the cobblestones,
Daubed invisibly: sweet, cloying remembrances.

Bottles left on a wall, tattered umbrellas, a
Pair of shoes in the street, filling with rainwater:
Girls' flat pumps, set apart——four or five paces. He

Treads
    the pulp
        of a grey

                        newspaper; fingers the

Keys
    and phone
        in the damp

                        pockets. (A paperclip . . .)

Shadow sweeping the road,
rounding the walker each
                    Space between the tall poles,
            buzzing with energy.


Tall white spire!    *Camarade!*    Lonely pyramidal
Form! I make my approach. Gables occlude you, but
No thin brick barricades baffle your paladin!
One more corner to turn—pattering lambency—
Then:

            Declamatory stone, listen. My grievances
Beg derision. A poor, stammering Ganymede—
Bleached by light that returns, broad and phlegmatic, from
That scored plate of your face—shivers and kneels to you.
Give me decorous scorn.    Flesh is immovable.

SPROUTS—
          (they jolt in vacancy, where the door was;
Pressed by lurid life in the dark reviving,
Light-ward, from this utterly dead potato),—

Scare me a moment.

## INDULGENCE

Something hides like a moth-eye watching us,
Grey against grey, waiting to flutter and flop,
Shaking its dust. At the window, can I drop

Into the night? the chimneys and the pavement—
The tides are fresh, without the self-involvement
We both suspect in each other and let pass.

# A COMIC SITUATION

*Each one of an affectionate couple may be willing, as we say, to die*
*for the other, yet be unwilling to utter the agreeable word at the right*
*moment; but if the wits were sufficiently quick for them to perceive*
*that they are in a comic situation . . .*

Meredith, *Essay on Comedy*

Though to the surface every quiet conveys
    A token of you, as the near
Is tenant always for the far;—
        That I should hear
The narrowing step, your key chirp at the door
    Again, already; even before
My having missed the touch of opposing days.

If our real pleasure issued spry and spry
    In passionate leaflets—every night,
Every day a thousand more,
        As green, as bright;
To blush at last, when blood in us dies down—
    Not wither like spring's crest and crown,
But each leaf turning golden by and by,

And living out our vigour—would that be best?
    Glow of the green is much to ask.
But some few, of a mottled kind,
        That like the mask
Taken for Agamemnon's, may be found
    Later—a leaf of gold in the ground—
Real; to be mistaken; to be kissed;

A solid proxy for a fading face—
      And for another face that fades,
Whose kiss it knows (or will have known) . . .
          One masquerades
Not for a hood against you, nor to be seen
      By you alone; but to get some green
Into the mottle, for a safer place.

Green communications run a risk
      I took before, by which I earned
The strong and level good I keep.
         And I have learned
To prize what dedicated failures win—
      But no new rhetoric wherein
To pose affection; no figures bright and brisk,

No steady sentence, no precise avowal
      To bring sedately what is meant
Up to the surface; all I have
         Is sudden assent;
Candour of silence, I hope; candour of touch.
      And, called upon for more—for such
Greenery as before—why do I growl

Some boring mundane thing, sooner than say
      A word you want, I mean, and both
Know—so well—the shading of?
         To tell the truth:
Because the burden buoyed upon the tone
      Consists; but every form I own
Calls for atonement after; heavy dray

Makes in the moment every opportune
      Delivery appointed, it may be;
The same load in a smoother carriage,

At a higher fee,
Might leave a cleaner track; and so to mend
    The method of conveyance I intend
Most earnestly; but when the nice poltroon

Determines to proceed against his flaws
        (No faults to you, in this one case),
It turns to hermitic flight from this
                Or that disgrace;
And you see nothing of the mind at work,
        And cannot tell that in the dark
Dim shuttles come over each night, with loving saws
        And grand confessions freighted.
Periods roll, beside you, soon
                Calumniated;—
Which more effective than one classic clause?

# THANKSGIVING FOR HUMAN
## ACCOMPLISHMENTS

There you are:
    And your strange regard:
        Across your things, just over there;——

Over the safe
    unlicensed area.

Give thanks
    for the erotic humanities.
To act under advisement—;
Reflect on usage, feel—like a phantom
    limb—the *usual* barrier.

Thanks even for the fears and fantasies
    of expertise—?

*

Now my streets contract
    To just this space of license that we make
    Between the door and closet.

Shall you and I rest a while
    in the warm depression?
Enjoy the minute missed,
    not turn to stay it—?

Blessing or curse, that *easy* never does it?

Give thanks
        for the taint of Fall:     no countermand,
No return to the First Age, any good
Without the relish of
                an art applied—

The theoretic sense     half understood
        And dignity of the sense
                of indignities.—

And may they be most wretchedly condemned
                Who make the attempt.

## CONDOLENCE

Sly cowardice
    in the face
Of death.
       I missed
         the dying;—

A failure of good manners, lapse
                Of *savoir faire.*

Secreted;
    any trace?
Heavy breath?
      though not
        quite sighing.

I recall the loitering, now—perhaps—
            Beyond repair.

Any solace secret too;—
    my reach
Lightly slides across you,
    lying
Still.——Like the water
    up the beach;
But sleepy fingers move replying.

# 'LOVE, GUILT AND REPARATION'

(*Melanie Klein*)

And what else *is* there? Loving in one's fashion;—
    Guilty? In ways that cross nobody's mind;—
One offers penalties in recreation.
    But your economy is not like mine.

Another may be slow to recognise
    Legalities of Love—such as one's own;—
Seeing themselves, through, as they think, your eyes,
    May feel for it, and say they can find none.

Outside communion, Guilt. Were it understood
    That under cover one is always paying
For inside sins;—and trying to make good
    With recondite Repairs: a kind of praying,

Just carried on, with hope, against the odds.
    My love to Caesar. But *these* debts, if they are paid
To shady creditors—the Household Gods—
    And not to you, is no atonement made?

## CUPID AND PSYCHE

He has hidden his face     and begged     for the room to be dark

And felt
        the hot drop on the skin,
                uncertain of provenance:

And felt
        that if light were burning,
                then she would find

No boy any more,     but a snake,     a lodger in murk.

The things I brought for gifts
    to whom and whom
It never concerned; which now I nurse,
Celebrant *solus*
    in an empty room;

Or follow—wispy in the air;
Palpitating in low sun;
       Fluttering over the slates just there;——

And I go after,
    blind;—
The trump Fool:
    and beneath,
Wake in the spreading pool.

Again the roof
    above the road:
Twilit—as then, at four or five,—
       But now, it may be, eight or nine;

I find I wander to the brink again,
Hoping again to reach your house from mine.

Poems of the epic cycles
I hate—

Nor may delight
In footways trodden by the crowd.

And I despise those tales
Of straying lovers; one doesn't drink

From every well; I scorn
Everything common.          Lysanias!

You're pretty,
You're pretty:

—But even before Echo
Has finished repeating,

Someone tells me
He's spoken for.

## PERSEPHONE

She wanders in boredom,
The perfect concrete heroine;
Walks alone, playing it straight: profoundly dead.

Sad girl:
She was beautiful;
Her world was dark with a gold centre.

Down there, tonight, this lamplit evening,
Prurient eyes rest on the new girl,
Or perhaps on her beautiful raincoat with sexy buttons.

A dog,
Squatting in the dark street,
Was gazing above. (For gods, or witches' flight?)

Undisturbed, the half-expected rite.
The pale-faced heroine plays with pity.
He pulled her —— deeply —— through the floor.

A full moon rose in decorously grim
Fealty; but full of promise.     Into this
Bile-dripping, heart-heavy frame

She gleams like oil,—like Jupiter's eyebeam,
Searching down into the dark.—And I'm
Oddly unstartled by the headlong kiss.

(Shall we speak about the weather? The mist,
      Its low-down lick,
         where the sheep are lying
      In cloudy peep,
         beyond the dying
Boughs, that are like the rivers along your wrist?)

Fold me entirely, root and rake-rustle, as
      Tight as you may inside
        this bloodless hide,
This echoing round with you, austere and blushless.

You come with a new and plausible pretence,
   Titan! to me
      (to the buckram-boarded sciolist),
Small before your blandishments.——
      (You, the cool hand and cheek; you glaucous-irised.)

. . . Not the commission of that later Duke,
She of the curling hand
         and the tapering line of the toes,
But Venus-Aphrodite,
         star, the 'Bringer of Night',
Over the Palace neatly trimmed in white—
And monotonal front of Duomo
(*Ottocento*, free of all rococo . . . )

In a town of ruddy brown to match
      the light of an orange sunset,
The massive Istrian or Dalmatian white
Brings to sum the snow on Monte Acuto.

     With Hesperus above,
         unglimmering, it declares
Also a continuity with stars—
In stone, secretion of the wave, descending.

PLANET!—collection of the wave ascending—
Of thee shall I be mindful,
     and of another song.

Why to the crisis? Sight, or hand,
    In service—making sure, less sure?
Not overlook but understand
    Should be the rule. Fixing on your

Eyes or mouth or wrist—I pause,
    Attending; coming close, maybe,
To a plausible crisis, when each draws
    Close to the other's reality;—

Do you know better—what sound that is?
    Grasshoppers in the undergrowth?
To tense it into sentences
    Could be a chance to hurt us both;—

And all the spoken words, yours even;
    Even of those I don't confess
My reading. They (so freely given)
    Stood for unlikely tenderness.

Ask me a favour. Try my patience:
    Let me be of use, and prove
How much I mean these implications;—
    Push, and something has to move.

# CLORIS AND LYSANDER IN
## A SHADY GROVE

### I.

There comes again that animal
      affluence, up to the mouth;
That pressing exhalation from the centre.

The stream of it rides over
      the instrument of the voice ——

It catches,
    he does not know when it will catch,
Like a wind blown over a leaf
    when it bucks and flicks;
And then there is a whimper;—

    Or like the carpets in Keats;
And then there is a waving kind of moan.

### II.

Say, in a shady grove the lovers lie.
The boughs of a laden fig tree modulate
Bodily shakings
      up against the trunk.

The youth communicates an intent to die.
It has come to be very plain the shepherdess
Feels able to continue as she is.

He cannot last any longer;
                    he is close to the end.
It is impossible he can go on living.


### III.


He can see the capacious structure of a death.
It takes the form of just whatever type
Can answer to the need, a positive
Containing negative; instantaneous.

The baker's tomb at Rome, dark cylinders
Boring inward, past the travertine,
To nothing: mechanism, to no end.

Order, with all motion at minimum.

It may be like the keel of a ship, capsized.
Around it goes the white stone peristyle,
          Socketed     at regular intervals,
The entries rounding off
                    into the darkness

Inside of which it is likely nothing moves.


### IV.


She would like the boy to promise not to die.
She cannot see why
                    to him it is so hard
To be so different from what he loves.

# VERONA

Today your deep dark eye,

Stripped of the veil
      (with that tinge, or
*Tint*,— pink, heavy and sensual),
                watches;——
   Follows me round that cincture
Of semicircular rounding Roman arches.

Lady, with your towers and triangles!
   Mermaids' tails on the skyline;
With your black bishop and your bitter wine;
   Your carnal stone;

The bands in the brickwork;

ROME ON THY BROW
         *and on thy wrists*——
Bright by day
        and lunar by night,
Lady, I like thee wet-slabbed in the darkness.

                *

You may not remember; we met once before.
I was struck by that red and white, the luxury
Of a sluicing gloss, a pink
        companionable presence.

Do you remember, we made small talk
   About your BIG DOG,
Whose sepulchral monument I much admire?

I know that *Romeo*
Is secretly not your favourite,
The *Gentlemen* certainly not—
(Or I might think less of you).

When swallows sweep over the squares at dusk
The blackening tapers on darkening blue
With newer elements burn the same
Fires, at the same old crowded
    Altar
    High over
    The river—
Where there is now the Museum of Archaeology.

*Catullus most I reverence.*

And let me again make mention,
    Lady, of your BIG DOG,
Who was the patron of Dante.

Why else bring *these* to *those*
      (lips, eyes and lips)—
Or think to press back the hand in the loosened hair,
If not to compromise mere rulerships:—
Press and kiss *that*,—
      lay sovereignty bare

Oneself, to be so agitated too,—
Under indulgence,
      modifying each?
Facing off mind to mind, deciphered through
The face;—the still more real thing
      out of reach?

Would you? I don't. So how apologise
For my unvoiced responsiveness? You matter—
You mean—but what?
      Is it legible in the eyes,
Lines of the mouth? Is it one with them?
      The latter,

At times I think:
      all *that*, is you;—all *this*,
Myself, I regret, unlovely.
      As my thought
Makes little pressure till its emphasis
In words—where, in the fact of it, hangs caught

And held all singularity it had,
Otherwise indistinct—
      your mind I feel,
First, in things said;

     then guessed in things unsaid;
But in the found form, there, it is most real—

There you are realized.
     In what I see
A couple of feet, a couple of feet away,
The claim of it is also real to me;
Which *is* my thought,
     no matter what I say.

And so not every thing has found expression
Sufficient for the daring.
     As, outside
The curtained window, somewhere in the garden,
A bird sang something,
     and a bird replied,

Just now, at dawn
     (when I am recalling you),
And I try, but cannot plot them over space—
Directions, intervals;—
     I can't construe
Our bearings, even mine; a hopeless case.

Upset
    by dissolution of the body,
I ignore more news
    of the human form in pieces.

———————————————

*Giselle*, Act One. Exuberance of the image
In maintenance of line,
                ascetic grace.
I am satisfied with surface. Talk about
Human Resources.
               *Probity of the art*—?
Inside, outside. The person in history—
Materials co-terminous with itself.

———————————————

The curtain falls in absolute silence.
The heroine dead.

          It is a strange distress
To watch the body
   amid the formal panic

And come to feel the tenuous thing—again
   vague and vagrant—

Has slipped away during the mimed alarm.

Not quite at the proper moment;
   in the time it takes
              to sense the rinsed,
              alien presence there.

# DISPARITIES

*Pontormo's Deposition*
(*Santa Felicita, Florence*)
*&c.*

*Each wound of His, from every Part,*
*All, more at home in her owne heart.*
CRASHAW

Fill the space around with colour;—
Makes the matter forfeit duller,
    Heavy in the floating dyes.

What to fix upon: the woozy
Figures, tinted gold and rosy—
    Or the face with lidded eyes?

One in faded green, like rotting
Flesh (the liquid standing, clotting,
    Still within; the life extinct);

Then the nine—men, boys and women:
Sky, blood-orange, lime and lemon;
    Musical, and poised, and prinked—

Rhythms of the fairy-story,
Daylight from the clerestory;
    Or, passed pain. Whatever it be,

*Miserere, miserere,*
Give us latitude to spare a
    Throb for foreign sympathy.

*Stabat Mater* (Pergolesi)

Comes—unruffled, cool, and hazy
  Round the sense—to help condole;

Making ready (*pertransivit*);
Making ready to conceive it:
  Finding out some ready hole.

*Contristatus*—and the lesson
Isn't simply of 'compassion';
  There, inside the drapery,

Daggers through the soul are passing,
Horrors yoking and amassing:
  He supremely *not like me*.

Virgil, *Aeneid* VI

The fiend again. I have no choice;
    I shudder and shrink, am pale and weak,
And what is mine within my voice
    Vanishes, though I must speak.

Vicar to this blithe deity,
    I don't lie still,—against deep force
Rave like a bacchant, shake to be free,
    Till I gape: I am bridled like a horse.

The words swill round ambiguously;
    My truth is bundled up in jest:
And so the god-beast Irony
    Drives in the spurs beneath my breast.

The Castrati are marching tonight:
                    from the hills they come,
Lumping ungainly bodies
To the place of congregation.
                    Tottering legs,
                    Toppling trunks,
                         And the *little heads* . . .

The trees have been cut back.
The crown of each stumpy poll
          Sprouts honorific garlands;
A dumb witanagemot,—closing,
                    Inside a circular grove,
The craning prodigies     hooting at half-Diana.

They hold     their Dark Assembly.
Sporadic strains of warble
                    from them issue—
Holding the birds stupid
                    in the untrimmed boughs.

Breathless again in the boskage,
How the Countertenors
Peer at their ancient problem!
From their beds they have come,—
                    the Masters of Achievement,
     Of DIFFICULTY SUBDUED.——

The Castrati are marching tonight.
                    Unearthly quarry.

Frankly, you seem
Rather too dim
To be, on principle, sincere.
And I wonder

If you are really
Quite so silly
As to pour forth in automatic candour.
No; I fear

You fall between two stools,
And we take each other for fools.

## PASTORAL OBSERVATION

O when wodwoses
Blow their noses,
    All the birds
Break from the trees;—
But the bumblebees,
    Undeterred,
Nuzzle within dog roses.

You come indoors to me; the trace
    Of the air outside—a fresh scent—lingers
In your hair and over your face:
    I can feel the cold wind on your fingers.

This evening I am out myself,
    Alone. Thick fog along the river;—
I see the better. But still, does half
    The sense go missing? Have I ever

Ascertained that hemisphere—
    That sphere:—that it matches mine? The mist
Evolves in quiet suspension here,
    Over the lawn; the oak-arms twist

Into and out of it, placidly,
    Opaque in it; sunset glowing through
The auburn of a linden tree
    With auburn light. Imagine two

Dubious circles ahead of me,
    Quivering on the undersides:—
The spanning arches liquefy,
    Rounded in water where it slides

Under them: bars of window-light
    Wriggle on that swaying layer,
Dulled by the mist; orange and white,
    Still glassy. Your not being there

Is felt most strongly at times like this:
    Guessing at you can modify
The aspect of exterior place,—
    As a mist, a purple evening sky,

Or a full moon's light can, on the stone
    Of too familiar buildings: here,
For example, last night — walking home
    At leisure, late. Chardin, Vermeer,

Had power to turn the variant play
    Of light to 'tactile values';—so,
In a special sense, do you. One may
    Hanker to weigh the auburn glow,

To stroke the purple, lick the mist;
    And these will not be caught or held
(The fool found out with the empty fist);
    The trick will trick or be dispelled.

But you in whom they also find
    Responses may be touched;—I might
Have reached around.—And the turning mind
    Inside there, like a trick of light.

Bactria sights you
Between taut bows.

The Persian opponent
From plated mount

Beheld you; the wintery
Hordes of the Getes,

And Britain with painted
Chariots, saw you;—

And India, pummelled
By Asian waters.

*

This cloak is the fourth
I have woven for war.

May he die, that man
Who was first to break

From the blameless tree
The rampart's stake;

Who wrought the horn
Through howling bone

To bellow out
Its dismal sound.

*

But tell me, doesn't
The breastplate hurt

Your tender arms—
And that heavy spear

Your gentle hands?
But better this

Should hurt you, than
Some girl, with her teeth,

Should give your neck
Marks, to my grief.

*

When Vesper induces
Bitter night

I kiss the weapons
You left at home;

Then I fuss, when the bedding
Lies uneven,

And grieve that the birds
Delay to call dawn.

(The whine of my new puppy
Is a comfort. She takes *your* side.)

*

In the winter nights
I work at your clothes,

Sew panels of purple
Wool for your cloak;

Learn where is that river
You are going to conquer;

How far those horses
Can go without water;

From my painted chart,
Where is cold, where is hot;

*

And what wind bears
Sails back safe
To Italy.

# THE CLUNCH PIT

*Ely / Cambridge / Orwell*

A line of chalk
across the land,
left by the once warm sound:
                    from here
it runs down, in a shallow band,
about as far as Buckinghamshire;
and the other way, up to the Wash,
                    where the zone
borders the beds of brown
          'carr-stone',—
and the belt of ferruginous
          'green-sand',——
the chalk to the wetness
                    dropping sheer.

Think of the chapel at Ely:
                    chalk,
from such a hollow,
made to serve
                    *Our Lady*;
lined up,— each tender stalk
reared to a kink, like a pulsing nerve;—
                    to canopies
nodding into ogees,—
                    ( . . . prowlets
of rococo doges—
                    slits
          wide gaping—,
          beak of the hawk . . . )
fruits, and foliage, fret the curve.——

——From chalk was made
  remembrance
of Bishop Alcock,——
    overhooded
by a Tudor Gothic spinney, dense
with crusting pinnacles,——
    a wooded
clatter accreting
(like the sound
    of citterns
strumming above and around);——
the solid clunch of the muniments
  dangled in shadow,
    heavy-loaded.

Far from the Bishop's towery brambles
  built on palates
    agape in the air;
from the Lady's nods
and nodes and tendrils
(headless figures clustering there);——
  quite another thing, the arch
    of the chancel
in Great St Mary's Church—
and the arches along the nave:——
    the spandrels,
and ribbons hemming above to the square;——

because here, the tracery ornament
  in daggers and foils
  and medlar-star
(or comxcomb of the pomegranate),
  secure, too high
  for thumbs to mar,

         is simple
         and solid.
         the lines
are clean;———the face of it takes
a waxy sheen,—
The pattern a sense
         of the deep, sharp print,
caught between bare wall
                           and voussoir.


Hard to the clime the fine chalk isn't:—
you look at the stuff
and you feel it would split
         with a knock;—
stone to festoon, bedizen,
         fuss;
a hard scrape effaces it.
Here at the crater, where the lime
made *this* from the life another time
         left,—
like bleaching bones, the lines glisten
in light, where the tracks ride down the pit.


Where the ground—under the grass—
was plated
deep with it, we
         can sit on the grass
at the uppermost lip—legs over;—
and seated—
         (thus)—
                  can look out far across
the fields: brown stretches, and yellow veins
where the rape is flowering,
         and the greens,

                    dark and light . . .
and the excavated
bowl beneath—as when you toss

                    a blanket:
the creases are all in motion;
ridged and covered quarry-lines
and the powdery lines of boots' erosion
                    plunge and skim,
and the pit declines
to where the rabbits are cheerfully
          browsing in the scrubby lea,—
bed, one time, of a tropical ocean;
                    filled; cut out for the tracery;———

## i. Prepared Confession

I recall the long night—the passage unguarded;
seeing it simple and sharp
and the whole thing possible and impossible;

and your one low, telling word—
the quickly-forgiven breach of peace,
recovered in a moment, without time lost—

look by look, *lie by lie*,—
former life by former life
forgotten, not joined,—

falling in one evening to the spaces
in which our sights converged;

and for us two (and for my instruction) the play was open,
and gave occasion for the caitiff vows of an earnest lover;
and was played out;
and was parodied sweetly within by the silent cynic.

We parted and were sorry;
and the third day you came again, remarking on the weather,
and collected your belongings;
and waiting in the black car was your father.
And I have come again without you, to walk in the rain and the snow
(whose falling is right on cue).

And I was bound to resent your loss—
the dull deliberate end
you produced as from the pocket of a coat;

and then the promise and the flop together were covered in retrospect.
You said you were busy.
And I recall that bilious and unconvincing laugh.

I'm aware of no shortcoming in my condition of soul.
But I look for the contribution of the flesh,
and the knees of a god to clasp—
no more.

## ii. Another Prepared Confession

I accept the blame, so lightly imputed;—
closer than water to earth . . .

To the falling rain's the only prayer I make,
who am encased in the viscid life;
brown as a guilty weapon
hidden under brightening water;

am glimmerless, furred, and fibred:

I pretended all was well;
the less said, the more the people inferred;

I considered all the options,
and settled for a long night with shame, the watcher of faces,
and saw it was time to peel the shimmering heart.

I accept the accepted tales:
the frozen rigorous head;
the betrayal of loves;
the solution of sex;
the imperfection of the lover,—
and the death intervening. (*Tant mieux.*)

### iii.  To Pylons

I have begun to see the broad insideless pylons
    by the motorway's side:

bad immodest angels upright and full outspread:
    bobbined or looped at the tips of their pinions:
    and the wires conveyed in cleanly order, without deference or
delegation:

they are chilly structures, made of blank
    hieroglyphic assertion, without passion,
conducting force for a million humdrum operations, over insouciant
landscapes.

We have seen, on our way, the crooked church-spire rise
    to an apex out of place, in *dark,*
                *diced,*
                *sombre*
                *lustrous*
        and *twisted* leads,
not unlike the dark hide of the dover sole, contorted over hot iron:
leaning along a blanket of dulled anaemic cloud-cover touched with
evening,
    as the fishmonger's ice-gravel is touched a little with blood:
but these titatinic and
    most veridical splay-forms metallic
have no blood, and will not yield; and will not make
        many supplications;

I have seen, also, the peaks    of dark and rusty brown,
    and the high plains    of dark and purple brown,
    the scrubby heather, like dry blood:
and these four-footed towers, they have no blood, but only electric
cargo;

and still are bright; and they will not compromise:

and also I have seen cut over the hills, by the road, the low stone walls,

   sharp-shadowed   in the morning sun:
      and   in the evening sun:
and the small thin trees, on the bright hillside, sharply shadowed
   vertically below:
   slots in the turf, symmetrical top to bottom:
but those sharp shadows, intimating roots, are not so sharp
   as the cages of high steel lattice shooting cables down the country
   like Francis and the laser-beaming seraph,
each with beatific arms in rigid austere extension.

Like every minor god they have
   an aspect sinister, among their several aspects;
they appear like the sorceror Rothbart over the neurasthenic lakes;
   and over the pulverous etiolated road-lanes
   rise like river-*numina* steering us;
they roll out over the hills in a cranky chain-bridge of six-armed apparitions:
   the series of emanations:
      and emanations of emanations:
the forms of endless multiplying
   divinities in steel, the bearers of wires.

   O steel divinities of many arms,
     of current power that are
   *transmitters*
   *conveyers*
   *intelligences*
   *wardens*
your passages recurving over the farms,
over the heath the colour of dry blood;

the slopes of rapeseed, yellow, tractate, combed as a fringe of
blond hair:

Electrical Pylons, for this lovely grouping
                              regrouping
                              further regrouping manifold
                              resolution into simple chains
        I make this offer of hymnody in thanks.
Deliver me from the terror by night,
                              and preserve us.


I have seen the dark bare upland lurch above the road;
the crooked spire rise to its point in twisting leads,
        like the black and somewhat shining hides of the dover sole;
and I have seen the sharp-lit edges of dry stone walls,
                many times,
                many days:
                              and all these I have noted.


Anonymous frames: o chic hard-headed cenoptaphs:
demonic samurai passing power
        on slender fancy crinolines of steel!
give fancy to the ways of my goings
with alternative motions, which are not open to me,
but are open to the mind that tends along them:
bring us to positive knowledge of the things that have been made
necessary:
                                        and from
                    the slackness of acceptation,
                    luke-warmness of accidie,
                    all idleness of sentiment, and of opinion,
                                        graciously preserve us.

Pink light fills the face of
　white Palladian marble.
　　　Deepening blue; sun slid
　　　burrowing under the lid.

Yesterday now like a forecast
　storm that never presented:
　　　Less than this shape in the pink
　　　shine; though a fracture, a chink

Somewhere, lets the bulb-light
　through, and that face, and the figure,
　　　Ruffling into the eye.
　　　Slight,—immaterial? Why,

Now, should it shy from a gleam of
　white in the dusk? The pilasters
　　　Candid, the capitals carved;
　　　spiralling animals halved:

Caught in the ashlar surface.
　(Shells, once pulpy at centre,
　　　Sected, suspended—*discrete*—
　　　roughen the silvery sheet.)

I, when a sleep intervenes, and
  day, but not this, returning,
     Brings no more the same,
      (nor any *more* than before),—

May, to sustain that delicate
  flicker, made gross in absorption,
     Try to recover this slow
      consonance bullying clocks

Spell for us; try to rehearse this—
  *misapprehension?*— the catching:
     Several hours, and you,
      tightening into the past.

# BEFORE THE WAR

*Vignette from Aeschylus*

'CHRYSELEPHANTINE',       with the silk,
The dyed-in-crocus
                spilling all around her

White skin ready against the silk
The soaked-in saffron
                falling from the white

All there waiting for the wash
Of a sun-dark crimson     beach-wave over the top
And spreading at the rim like a tassel fringe.

## DOUBT

My doubt has manholes ladder-lined for two.
It's damp down there. The files are all corrupted.
You may find something, somewhere, where I dropped it;
But it may not mean anything to you.

And it may be hard to pick out from the silence.
Well, I suppose you have years and years to spare?
Shall I fill them up with dulcimers and violins,
To clang and moan the sweet way to despair?

This bowl,
    which I carry always,
Packs in
    the pillowy lobes

Like the flesh
    of a hard-cased fruit,
Greased
    with a cover of blood-blotch.

And this bolt of bronze I poise
In my right hand
    is a cast current,

Cold, like a prow to cleave
The pulp, where sparks
        used to think.

## A DREAM

You are hiding in a cupboard, because afraid
Of death. Thump on the woodwork: big, bare, greyed
Foot against the pine, enjoiningly.

In every death the flesh is changed. How much
With this new creeping death it grows
A thing, a lump in the sink,

Filling the brain with touch, as the flesh of those
Who leave us and go on living
Cajoles the mind with the desire of touch.

I have turned away
     from a sunset I can see
In ranks of windows.
      The long terrace faces
Into the banded colour and onto me;
Brick surface dark
     around brilliant panes.
     *Æsthesis*!


The pink is bright, because the space behind
Is not . . .
     (—To think, like this,
     of the inside:
     *Eros.*—)
I am close;
     there are spots of mould on the back of the blind.
Do exhalations thicken over the glass,


Suppose:
     when they, awake or in several dreams,
Release their humid air to affront the cold
Of this outside,
     until the liquid streams
To the sill—?
     *Ethos*;
the real—they slip your hold.

Orange lights, in the dark,
Roll out over the contours
Of the indiscernible surface.

As on that superannuated plane;
The late-night landing, watching
The lights of Honolulu and the lights
Lining the runway.
                          In the humid air,
In the American car,
Hurtling past the little orange points
Shaking in the warmth;
                                    passing
Through the invisible wideness of plantations
Wafting a sweet decaying smell,
Brown and moist,—a cloying smell
Of rich pineapples ripening in the soil.

     Waiting
          to mount
               the black hill;
     Winding
          around
               the black bends;
     The stop to open the gates.

Climbing up the driveway, past the dark
Witchy masses of the mango trees,
If there were a bump, it would likely be
An unlucky frog gone under the hot tyre.

And waiting for the warm metallic clunk;
For grasshoppers and crickets. Hollowness,

Warm, of the wooden treads; the alarm's
High note:——four beeps, and a long reassuring fifth.

Then the metal bed frame,
Sticky in the heat;
With the cheap sensation
Of a mosquito net.

Waiting for a dawn with genuine roosters,
The view of the ocean,
The dust on the furniture,
The caking of the sugar,
Dead geckos amid the imperishables.

Centipedes,
six inches long,
trail down,
Dangled on reddish rafters:    and might drop.

Coiled ones on the carpet lie
Dead of the poison,
like dried-up
Bean pods, crackling in the hand, that grew
In the vicinity of yellow flowers.

Concrete; the guavas' decomposing pulp,
With a sickly smell,
a dull crust from the sun;——
Volcanic dirt: a few steps
And your feet are red.
This long, rocking taedium

Of worn upholstery
And grey plastic.

Between the stars and the crickets,
          Behind the shuffling bulk
          Of the dark immobile cloud,
There are dark bodies perching in the dark.

Adults could detect their privy places;
Stooped with a smile at the restaurant railings,
Indicating from the the wooden deck,—
          In the languid space
          Before dessert.
          (Some kid in summer
Employment;—but she counted.)

Out of the branching capacities;
Out of the night-black brain,
The plangorous inhuman calls,
Foreign as music on the clavichord,
Issue, like the cries of dead children.

Even the kitsch I cannot quite recall,
          Impossible not to surmise,

          Is almost dear
            and almost alien;
              always
          Lit by continual
            but inconstant
              sense

Of presence,
          Known and (it seems) half noticed then:

The wavering of crickets,
                    stars,
                    lamps,
And the rich smell of hot rubber in the car park.

Pines begotten high on Pelion's peak
Some time are said to have swum the liquid waves
Of Neptune, to the tides of Phasis, bounds
    Of Aeëtes;——

It was in the days when those young men elect,
Hard oaks of Argive vigour,
           canvas set
From Colchis, to bear off
             that golden skin,

Ventured to overcourse the salty sea
In a quick stern, sweeping
Cerulean plains
         with blades of fir;

For whom that Goddess who preserves
The turrets
Of city-summits

Built that water car,
To glide on the light breeze,
Joining the pine contrivance of keel's curve.

That was the craft instructed
    First with its course
Amphitrite, before those days unwrought.

And when it rent with its beak that windy sea,
And the water, wrested by the oar-beat, grew
    Grizzled with spume,

From the ocean's glittering gurgitation
Nereids put up
Faces emergent, goggling at the monster.

At that time—and no other—
Mortals saw, with the very light of their eyes,

    Salt-water Nymphs:

Forms denuded;
Far as the nipples
Extant from the silvered surge.

Vapour was grey between the walls,
                    Rolling——
Between the corners; and the cold flapped.

Grey like a cygnet
                    Slowly revolving—
        The clouds amassing.

                    *

The air was damp and like a leper's bell
Sent ahead.        The pressure fell
        And then the sky
Loosening into the rain; and the purple clouds,
With the mass of the mind, began to be let down.

But inside beaten windows, over town,
They go to dinner early, as
                            the sky

Loosening into rain, the purple clouds,
And the press of the brows, come down.——

                    *

The clouds, purple as rain-wet slate,
Fell to a frankness;——fat, loud drops
        Brought against the stone,
        Poured on the lagoon,
The higher places nerving for the storm.

But when it came,     tight as an angry word
Repeated without conviction;
          Sick;     a lame bird;—

Shards of water, as from a wing,
It shook. Or like a rug;—
                                             the sky
Yellow with it. (It could only be
          A *civilized* malaise.)


                         *


                              These days,
The grum fish lurk on a level,
Yards below the plague-wind and the sun,
Where the black vessel used to glide,
Slight as a plume of curly-headed fern.

Low cloud-slivers skid across the hill
Where dry headstones, like rutted carious teeth,
Scrape the lurid alabaster flesh
     Of a draggling dusk: an old, cut
Plum, darkening, softening, at the edges.

Inland, the groupers in the lake
Push around their fat patrician jowls
Untroubled by the fit come over the leaves.
There are moorhens in the eaves.


                         *


'*And then mine understanding was led down
Into the deep sea ground;*
                              *and there I saw*

*Hills and dales, all green and moss-begrown.*
*With many weeds, and gravel, it was strown.'*

    But like a bloody caul
      The corals
    Web the faces
      Of the corbels.

    Gothic saints
      Loom out to frighten
    Passing nereid
      And triton.

*

The sun performing summer arches
Over the summits, their white cover
    Leaks a little, and stays.

The light continues turning over
Shining needles of the larches,
    Into the dampening days,

Until the passage of the sun is low,
And the clouds are pink with snow.

*I am weary of myself, I abhor and buffet mine own self, that
not more, not more fully do I repent, Lord. O Lord, I repent,
help Thou mine impenitence.*

I.

I step out
In pyjamas
Onto the plank
Over the spinning rotor. Who will applaud
This gamble?
    Will it give or hold?    It takes

No more than a stumble: a moment's doubt:
If any looker-on
                Should shout
To wake me from the muddy bank.

II.

To birch away
With penitential besom
    Every *gaucherie*,
    Every solecism;—
Put in place, a regular, purging
Quietly
Out of sight—before
Too late.
    The sins pile up at such a rate.

## III.

Committed to the jurisdiction
Of canon law—sincerely, I
Submit.
    I have not tried to be unacceptable.
Neither do I haggle for a welcome.
The lack is of power, not scruple, or shame. Come buy.
I blow my slug-horn at the cloudy sky.

---

*All pay themselves the compliment to think*
*They one day shall not drivel . . .*
                    YOUNG

---

The sluicing wash of a wide blue coverlet, spread
Sharp at the feather-bed edges;
                              yellow valance;——
The dyed, live
              tranches of bounded colour;
Live and quiet light
                    —bryght
                    brode cheldez—
Etched
        over, under,
        in scrubbed grisaille;——

Far-off blue castle, four blue cornering towers,
Every tower with a hat in bright red clear,
Acute:

        For centuries, all of this was more
Distinct than any earthly thing regarded
'Darkly' through unpainted windows; i.e.,
These effigies,—this demon's upper face
Of two: head like a dark fig or a leg
Of lamb, gore-purple and stuck with a lurid fish-eye,—
These seeming saints,
                      were crisper than what passed,
If it passed, or the eyes lay, more than foot from the pane,
By the clear glass of those times, and the times succeeding.

The mullion christ-crossed frontages of later
Prodigy houses, high, diaphanous, still
Gave only a dubious vision—yellowy-green,
                              as under too much old varnish;

Bubble-freaked and flawed in the fabrication;
Views to be taken true from the leads alone.

Slim, easy as a weed, between the yellow
Heaven and red hell: blond lepidopterous Fay!
Interpreter of Light,——blue, very pale,
           Wings; and green; with a touch
           Of yellow; a purpure fringe,
Annulet-bored in blue, less pale, across:—
Debonair Archangel of the age of Skelton:—

Victorian hueless windows, even, in which
The true sights billow
           counter the passing gaze,
Spanned here with a standing wake, this gracing weam,
Caught into colour-rolling bows, deliver
              an image less exact
Than this display.

Did it strike them as more real when Henry the Eighth
Was still the slender young poet at the virginals?
To the present architectural tourist, is it?
To the cunning glazier, Barnard Flower, was it?
And what exactly is the matter here?

Stripes of lashes
      Left on the cheek,
Sticky as stains
      Of pollen — black
As the silky straps
      Against pale skin.

I.

Something ought to be said
  concerning Valerio Belli,
Carver in *pietre dure*;
  master incisor of hard stones.

Rock crystal——thinned
  and ground to panel or vessel——
He gave decoration with small drills,
  borrowing compositions

From various sources (some identified).

II.

Tension of eye—and of the hand—
  Tiny deviations from the still:

Clarity cut with form, to the white,
  Like foam on a surface too calm to have meant it.

III.

Diaphanous type projected in clean lines;
Antique bodies, naked or
  draped; the occasional papal
Bust in profile, bounded medalwise.

No spirit diorama, angel scene
Summoned in the globe; no company

Of little men grown up by chemistry
Inside the blown retorts.

He, the informer;—it,
    the form cut into the quartz;—

Entails the matter.

### IV.

Undulant curls of hem; edges where light
Glares on the shape it cannot clear uncaught.
Edges of cloth that wriggle down the robe—

Vermiculation of tidy gravity,
With each turn interposing another fold,
Supposition of plane beneath plane opposing;

    Semi-opacity grading.

But there, in the eddies: the lines of delicate pull;
Adhesion, to the figure, of the cloth:

Like sheets of gold leaf, laid, before the brushing;
Thin petals, in hot sun, over a finger.

### V.

    This very small and colourless plaquette:
    Put a back to it,
                Make it answer:
    Otherwise hold it free
        to the current space.

*Vicenza, May 2015*

Settled under force,—
    whereas before
Terraces like these
    laid under Rome
Were full of well contented citizens
Freely come for more sportive atrocities.

Is it better or worse,
    'on the question of righteousness'—?
Can we say *better*,
    now it is called an outrage?

———————————————

    Glowing bars
    of columns,
           set
    As fluent runs
    for the copper light

Medial, up between the sandy ground
And patent countervalency of sky:
These without mythos, literary life
Or character articulate in words
Articulated space and solid mass
In face of mind to face it.
              Fitting now
The proper human form, and human life
Proper,
    should be found these final bonds,—

Ill will banally sensible
                of coherence.

The meaning of the address is clarified.
Fitting a piece of being to the style,
They blow the even shafts away to rubble.

# SPEECHES

In the dark of the hall, the tall glasses
    shone like coins in a fountain;
the attitudes    of the candles
    being like little eddies,

and the coins themselves, which the tall
    glasses were like, red and white,
being otherwise like the two eyes
    at the far end of the dark hall,

that had a wet glitter, attending
    harder than I to the speeches,—
and in this shy light    were like
    sibilance in church responses

lighting up the words I fail to remember.

These sorry flowres,
Whose legs
Graze the dark leaves of personality;—

Occasionally their needes for love
Fill upp their veynes, —; —;
Wishing thy juce, and sad soveraigne showers.

　　But taste and dye.
　　(Then why not I?)

How could you reste from the wet thing, the
Long, long cheated promise?

Beautiful rectification of
This foreign love.——

Stand, unfinished world.

　　In my room
　　I soare.

The organ, like a silk flag in light wind,
Heard in the lulls, wavy beneath the voices:
Sound of quotidian labour, scheme of life?

Or the undulations of angelic care
Buoyant in the vaults, oil over water?
Oil in the machinery? Undecided.

When to know the miraculous from the banal
Is difficult; when, as in you, they join;—
To be ready | not to look | over one's shoulder?

## THOU ART OF PURER EYES THAN
## TO BEHOLD EVIL

The days of puncture—dusk—the nights of puncture.
  Calamitous flop,
    interminable trickle . . .
Despair in fixity,
    desperation at juncture.
  Affliction for the steadfast *and* the fickle.

The world is such a different place for others.
  The greater sadness
    of becoming fat . . .
Tenebrous degradation
    of old mothers;——
  And who takes great enough account of that?

Contradiction; ever the fact.—It mines
    Deep into the earth;—you cannot tunnel
        Under it;—its roots anticipate.

Its architecture fumbles to the light
    Whichever way you wander, and its spores
        Pursue you when you take the higher way.

Have commerce with your own hypocrisy.
    Know it; remember every furtive face,
        And make a treaty with the colonies.

Come, naughty one, say true.
Push—oh, we can do
Such things. Let's not be nice.

Then, faith, the dew rose
Over me, pointing the skin.
The rush within me blows

With the old, rogue wind     of Paradise;
Putting a sense of life in me.

## THE SHIPS

Months before
I took the ships
I leant under
The rusty bridge edge
That hurt the River
Just less
Than the judgement of
Her shaded banks.

# FOUR IMAGES

### I.

Over the dark plane
      dimpling into sight,
In the heat, lights
      are shivering on the shore.

### II.

From the walls of a hilltop town
      the summer night
With drops of orange
      pricked on blue and black
Quakes and wavers
      down still intervals.

### III.

——Or,
Figured across
      the species of a lake,
Stars that are barely seen
      relax and pitch.

### IV.

Yellow
breathing
spots
      on a starling's back.

# PIETÀ

The emotion of the stilled *pietà*
Is of control:

Animal sensation present
In structures of the soul—
The signs arisen
Out of framed feeling, edified dolours.

Control of the facial musculature,
And of the vocal cords—isn't
That the beginning of culture?
Dignity follows;

The first accomplishment
Is *sangfroid*.

*'a series of disgusts'*